CHRISTMAS ADAM

BY AMBER NOBLIT

ILLUSTRATED BY NATALIE SYTSMA

DEDICATION PAGE

Christmas Adam is Dedicated To

Kendra- my first friend! We had great ideas! Love you!

Philip-You are my Best Friend, Partner in Life, Love and Ministry.
Thank you for supporting my crazy ideas!

Justus and Hadyn- My two world changers!
Continue to Love Loud, embrace the broken and be the hands and feet
of Jesus everywhere you go.

In Loving Memory of a true God Given Friend
who pushed me to share our family tradition.
Jill Hamilton... "I did it!"

The day is slower than normal thought Sarah as she anxiously awaited the clock to strike 3:30. Christmas break was almost here. Mrs. Sawyer was very aware that the entire class was far too excited to focus on the normal studies; so standing at the front of the classroom she said, "Does anyone have a special holiday tradition that you can share with the rest of the class?"

Everyone began to talk at the same time. "Ok, ok," said Mrs. Sawyer, "One at a time please." Taylor lifted her hand and said, "My family always goes to Vail, Colorado and goes skiing!" Peyton raised his hand and said, "We go north to my grandparents for Christmas, and there is always snow!" One by one, the students shared about when and where they would open their gifts and what made Christmas special.

Sarah was so excited about class being over that she was not paying any attention to what the rest of the students were sharing. "Sarah, what about you?" Asked Mrs. Sawyer.

Sarah, knowing how excited she was, burst into the explanation of her story. "Yes! We have special traditions! Every year we go to my grandparent's house in Texas. We bake cookies; we watch Christmas movies; and we take homemade goods and cards to our friends on Christmas Adam!" Sarah said with such excitement! "Christmas Adam?" Asked Mrs. Sawyer. "What is Christmas Adam?"

All the class began to giggle. "There is no such thing as Christmas Adam! That is a made up day!" one student loudly protested from the back of the room. Sarah became very frustrated that no one was taking her serious and she blurted out "Yes there is! Christmas Adam is the day before Christmas Eve!"

At this the whole class went from giggles to full out laughter. Mrs. Sawyer, still very confused but intrigued, asked "Sarah, why do you call it Christmas Adam?" All of a sudden, Sarah found herself in a place where she had never been. Confused and embarrassed she searched for an answer. She thought to herself, "I don't know. It's just what we have always done! I can't tell them I don't know because they will laugh even harder! What do I do now?" Just then the bell rang! "Saved by the bell," mocked that same voice from the back of the room. As Sarah gathered her things, she was determined to have the answer when she returned from break.

That afternoon, as Sarah's dad was loading the car, he noticed the look on Sarah's face. "Sarah honey, is everything ok?" he asked. "Dad, are we a weird family?" Sarah blurted out. As he chuckled, he replied, "Well, I guess it depends on whom you ask." That was not the answer that Sarah wanted, nor did she appreciate him messing her hair up as he turned to walk back into the house. "Maybe the kids were right! Maybe Christmas Adam is a dumb day we made up. Maybe it's nothing to be excited about," Sarah thought to herself.

After 8 hrs of driving down the road, they were finally at Granny's house! As Granny opened the door, the warmth of the fireplace thawed Sarah's cheeks, and the smell of fresh baked cinnamon rolls filled her nose! "Granny!" screamed Sarah! "There's my girl! I have been so excited for you guys to get here!" Granny exclaimed as she pulled Sarah tight.

It didn't take long before the whole house was full of laughter and stories, as family came in from all over.

That night as Sarah lay in bed full of joy and surrounded by the love of family, she recalled the way the class laughed at her tradition. All of a sudden, she felt the happiness leave her, and sadness took over. She didn't like how it made her feel.

As Sarah fought tears, she heard someone moving around in the kitchen. She got out of bed, put on her slippers and robe, and went down stairs. Sarah quietly crept into the kitchen and was relieved to see Grandpa. "Sarah, are you ok sweet girl?" asked grandpa. "I guess," Sarah said with a pout. Grandpa pulled a stool out and said, " Hop up there kiddo and tell grandpa all your problems." Sarah smiled and climbed up in the stool. "Well, we were talking about Christmas traditions at school, and I don't know why we celebrate Christmas Adam." Grandpa leaned back in his chair and sighed. As he pulled his glasses off and rubbed his forehead, he leaned over to Sarah and said, "It is a very special Holiday; one that your granny taught me about. Maybe you should let her explain." Not happy with his answer but wanting to hide her disappointment she sighed "Yes, sir." She kissed Grandpa on the head and went off to bed.

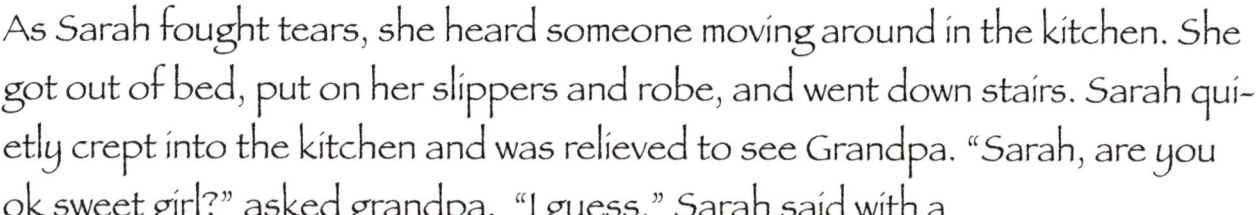

The next morning, Sarah got up early hoping to talk with Granny. She could smell the coffee brewing and knew that granny was up! Sarah took off down stairs to find Granny cooking in the kitchen. "Well good morning, sugar! You sure are up early!" said granny as she hugged Sarah. Granny had hugs that just made everything always feel better.

"Granny," Sarah said reluctantly, "Can I ask you something?" Granny stopped and looked at Sarah concerned by the tone of her voice. "Well, of course," she said, "What is it?" Sarah sat there for a moment trying to find the words; finally she said, "Granny why do we celebrate Christmas Adam? Is it some weird holiday that we made up? All the kids in my class laughed at me and even my teacher was puzzled at Christmas Adam."

Granny put the monkey bread in the oven and after pouring herself a cup of coffee sat down right next to Sarah. "What is Christmas Adam?" Granny repeated back as she gently brushed Sarah's hair out of her face. "Well my dear, it was a special holiday my sister and I made up when we were little girls." Before Granny could say anymore, Sarah interrupted, "So it is a weird holiday our family made up!"

Granny, understanding Sarah's frustration, pulled her close. "It is made up, but it is not weird; it is, in fact, my most favorite of all holidays," Granny said, and then she proceeded to tell the story that would change the way Sarah saw Christmas and the way Sarah saw God.

"When I was a little girl, our family would open all of our gifts from each other on Christmas Eve. Christmas morning was reserved for stockings and then Grandma's house. As my sister Kendra and I would watch the gifts fill up under the tree, we always wanted to open just one early. We asked our parents if we could open just one gift on Christmas Adam.

"Of course that was the first mention of Christmas Adam. We explained that Adam came before Eve so we should celebrate Christmas Adam as well. My parents laughed and explained that the word eve meant the night before, but Kendra and I did not care. Christmas Adam was already in our hearts, but for the wrong reasons.

"After Christmas was over that year, my parents came to us and said that we would be able to open the gifts from each other on 'Christmas Adam' if we could come up with a meaning for such a holiday. We thought about it and tried to be creative, but nothing came. And then one day, it happened."

"What happened?" Sarah whispered on the edge of her seat. "Well," Granny said "we were at VBS at our church. The whole week was about Creation. They talked about the Garden of Eden, the animals and the beauty of the earth. Then they talked about God creating man and how He named him Adam.

They also told us why God created man. He wanted someone to have a relationship with. Adam was more than an animal or anything else God had made. He was created in the very image of God. God would walk with Adam in the cool of the day; He loved him and took care of him. He even saw that Adam needed not to be alone in the garden and gave him a wife named Eve.

"Now Eve was tempted by the devil and both Adam and Eve ate of the tree that God had told them not to. God had to take them out of the garden forever. Before they disobeyed, there was no pain; there was not sickness or even death. Sin brought that into the world, and now Adam and Eve had to live with those things.

Many years later, God sent his son, Jesus, to die for the sins of man so that man could be in relationship with God just as he had created it to be.

"I remember sitting with my sister and talking about how Adam was God's first friend, and that God was more than just the creator God and God the father, but He wanted a relationship with us, like a friendship. At that point Christmas, Adam took on a whole new meaning. It would be the day we celebrated the gift of friendship in our lives.

"When we explained it to our parents, they loved the idea. The months leading up to Christmas were so much fun, coming up with ideas to make this day special! I remember that first Christmas Adam like it was yesterday. We made dozens of cookies and took them to all of our friends. There were notes that said that friendship is a gift from God. We laughed and sang Christmas songs as we drove from house to house. That night, Kendra and I exchanged gifts. We believed that the best friend given by God was each other. It was such a special time for me. I think the most special part of it all was my relationship with God had become so real.

"You see my sweet girl, to some, Christmas Adam may be a weird made up holiday, but to those who understand God given friendship, it is very special. We have passed that down to our children, and now they are passing it to you. Does that answer your question?" Granny said. Sarah smiled, and tears ran down her face. "Sugar, what's wrong?" asked Granny as she wiped Sarah's tears. Sarah replied, "I never thought about God wanting to be my friend, and I never thought about my friends being gifts that God had given me." Granny kissed Sarah on the cheek and got up to take the now golden gooey monkey bread out of the oven. She turned to Sarah and said, " He is such a good God."

The rest of the family begins to wake, and soon the house was full of laughter and talk of the preparation for that night's Christmas Adam celebration.

Sarah went up to the attic where she spent a lot of time playing dress up and looking at old pictures. She sat there for a moment and she began to pray, thanking God for all her friends and for all of the relationships He had given her. Then she asked Him to be more in her life than He ever had.

Sarah walked downstairs with a peace in her heart that was worth more than any gift that was under the tree, or anything she would find in her stocking the next morning. Friendship with others, and more importantly with God, was a priceless gift. Christmas Adam would from that day be known as Sarah's favorite holiday, and she would share it for the rest of her life.

The End

100% of the proceeds from "Christmas Adam" go towards helping empower this generation to live a life on mission through the discipleship efforts of One Loud Voice. For more information, please visit our website: www.oneloudvoice.me

CPSIA information can be obtained
at www.ICGtesting.com
Printed in the USA
BVHW010200141118
532948BV00002B/2/P